To . . . .

From . . . .

the delinquent fairy's thoughts on

exercise

lauren white

MQP
MQ Publications Ltd

INTRODUCTION

I'm Flo — the DelinQUEnT fAiry : "ExerciSE gURU ExtraorDinAire." PEople Often ask me How I mainTaiN my Perfectly Toned PhysiQue And

ASTOUNDING lEVEl of Fitness:
the Answer is in This Book!

I'll HappiLy run A maraThon,
cirCuit Train, do my PiLates Session
and Fit in A quick Swim — All befoRe
breakfAst...... tHen I wAke up.....

(dream sequence)

Remember : ExerciSE is Fun.
It's especiAlly fuN if You Are
muNching a mars Bar watching
SoMeone else do iT !

(ANyway ChoCoLate gives you
extRa Vital enerGy for the gYm !!!)

THis LittlE boOk is so pAcked
witH enerGy-BoOsting, Tummy-
tigHtening, PuLse-rAcing sTuff
You'll fEel Flushed juSt reAding
it!

JuSt remember the first Two
Golden RuLes of fitNess ———

⁎ AlwaYs cHeat wheneVEr poSsiBle
⁎ NeVer ComProMiSe yoUr digNity

Read On for the Rest..........

THE BENEFITS OF EXERCISE

shiny hair ....

glowing complexion .....

smug virtuous expression .

muscular torso (?!) ...

toned legs .....

plus general increased confidence

(or see "how to cheat" section ......)

FLo's MORNiNG JoG

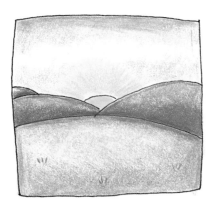

just   as   the   sun   is   rising...

... the alarm clock rings....

Flo awakes, stretches ...

. turns over and goes back to sleep...

TOP 10 DANGEROUS SPORTS
N⁰ 10

JOGGING

TOO PUBLIC

GAUGE YOUR FITNESS

POST-WORKOUT COLOR

SMUG

CAN MANAGE
a PRESS-UP
OR TWO...

IN
THE
PINK!

GLOWING
WiTH
HEALTH

NEEDS A
LiE - DOWN

CaLL
AN
AMBULaNCE!

THE
WISDOM
OF
FLO

.......don't tone up.........

. . . . . . just cover up ! . . . .

iT's THE Way you WALK !

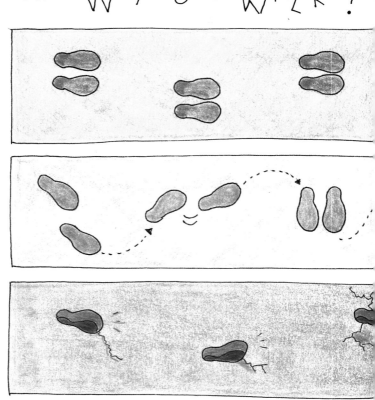

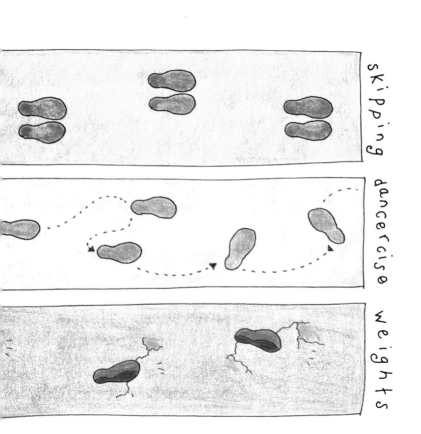

skipping

dancercise

weights

HOW TO CHEAT!
Nº 1

makeup for that "just left the gym" look.

Top 10 Dangerous Sports
☆ Nº 9 ☆

WEIGHT LIFTING

TOO HEAVY

Flo's quick fitness tips...

strap on baked bean cans for an all-day workout...

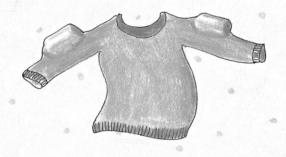

... result: really odd-shaped clothes!

THE ALTERNATIVE WORKOUT GUIDE

...... the warm-up .....

..........the bicycle..........

........the stretch and flex..........

the lift. . . . .

.......the marathon.....

. . . . . s t e p   w o r k . . . . . .

Top 10 Dangerous Sports

· N⁰ 8 ·

Swimming

TOO WET

GAUGE YOUR FITNESS

post-workout footwear guide......

NEVER SEEN
THE LIGHT
OF DAY

ONLY
FOR
SHOW

"RUNNING
IN"

"RUNNING
OUT"

"PHEW!"

R.i.P

HOW TO CHEAT !
Nº 2

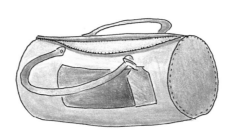

carry the right bag.

THE WiSDOM OF FLO

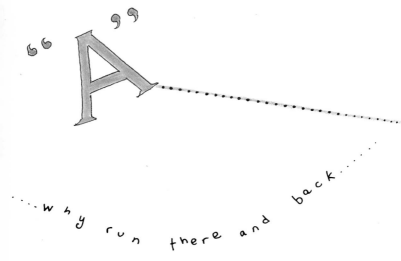

"A" ...why run there and back.....

...when you could just stay where you are?.......

" B "

Top 10 Dangerous Sports

✧ Nº 7 ✧

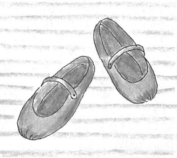

DANCE

TOO EMBARRASSING

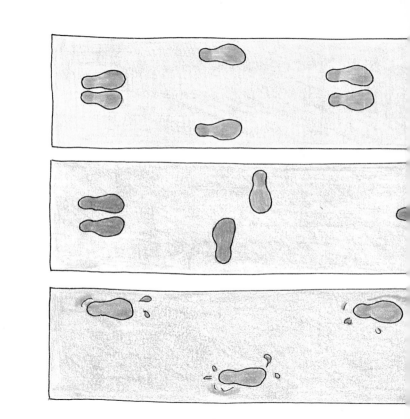

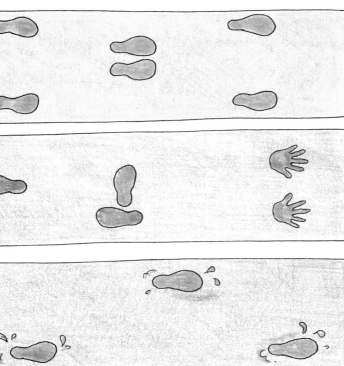

aerobics

yoga

x-country running

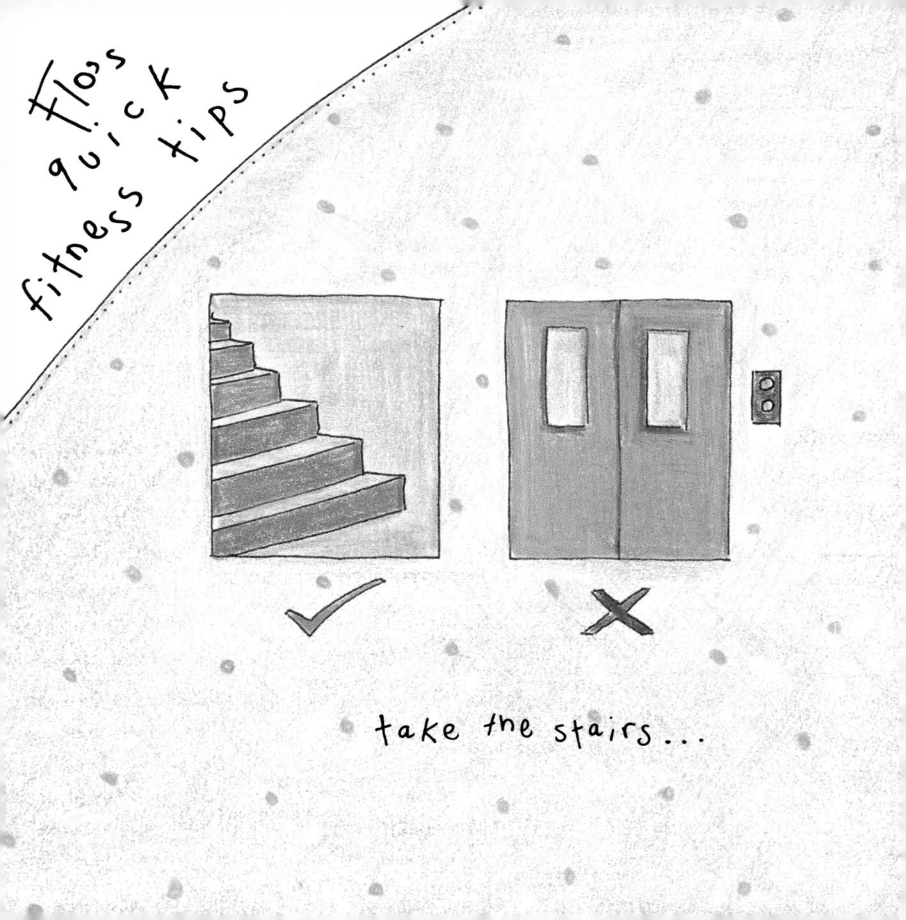
Flo's quick fitness tips
take the stairs...

...and some oxygen!

TOP 10 DANGEROUS SPORTS
☆ №⁼ 6 ☆

AEROBICS

TOO COMPETITIVE

THE WISDOM OF FLO

always judge a health club.........

.... by its cheesecake! ....

HOW TO CHEAT!
№ 3

the right clothes are essential

GAUGE YOUR FITNESS

post-workout   sounds!....

SHOW-OFF

JUST FOR
EFFECT

"I WISH I
WASN'T
HERE..."

FEELING
THE
STRAIN

SERIOUSLY
OVER-
DOING iT

SEND
HELP
NOW!

TOP 10 DANGEROUS SPORTS

✦ Nº 5 ✦

BOXING

TOO PAINFUL

Flo's quick fitness tips...

pick daisies one at a time : stand... bend... pick ...

... result ?... lots of daisies !

THE WISDOM OF FLO

.... it ain't what you do ....

............it's what you wear !.............

TOP 10 DANGEROUS SPORTS

* Nº 4 *

CLIMBING

HELP!

TOO HIGH

IN THE BAG...

designer label of course

jet-powered running shoes

pure white fluffy towel
(to drape casually around shoulders)

selection of lycra tops (to match the gym equipment)

chocolate (for energy)

ultra-effective deodorant

odor-eating socks

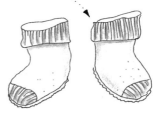

How To cHEAT !
№ 5

JOGGER

LTH

MUSCLE

DUMBELL

appear

interested....

Flo's quick fitness tips...

hook up your pedal power...

...and light up your life!

TOP 10 DANGEROUS SPORTS
⋆ Nº 3 ⋆

iN-LiNE SKATiNG

TOO RISKY

A TRiP AROUND THE GYM...

S . . . . . T . . . . R . . . . . E . . . .

T C H !

iNcReASE

ENDURANCE

FEEL THE

BURN!

B U i L D

STAMiNA

TOP 10 DANGEROUS SPORTS
* Nº 2 *

Y O G A

TOO BENDY

Flo's
quick
fitness tips...

abandon all labor-saving devices...

... shallow baths will do just fine !

THE
WISDOM
OF
FLO

.........in the gym.........

. . . . no one can hear you scream. . . . .

How To cHEAT !
No 6

HAPPY SMILES
HEALTH AND
FITNESS CLUB

Flo

carry the card.

Top 10 Dangerous Sports
✦ Nº 1 ✦

HULAHOOPING

JUST RIGHT

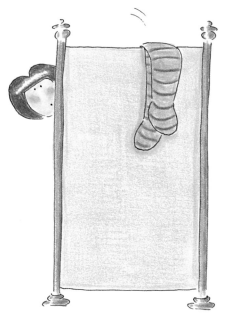

PEOPLE
eXeRCise To "KeeP THeiR FiguRe"...

I'D RATHER SWAP MINE FOR SOMEBODY ELSE'S!

Lauren White spent much of her childhood at the bottom of the garden involved in a fruitless search for a real live fairy! Many years later, up popped Flo: Lauren comments "You imagine a shy, delicate creature with shimmering wings and a bell-like laugh—I got saddled with Flo!"

Flo has an opinion on everything. She's mischievous, subversive, and likes taking a very wry look at the antics of mortals. Lauren has managed to capture some of Flo's thoughts on aspects of the human condition and set them down in this little book.

Flo and Lauren live in the village of Cranfield in Bedfordshire, England, with Michael (mortal) and Jack (canine; terrified of Flo), where Lauren spends her spare time sketching, playing the piano, and adding to her collection of Victorian pixie lights (53 at present) by scouring antique shops and fairs. She has produced gift books celebrating life, books of spells (with Flo's guidance), and her designs for Hotchpotch greetings cards are sold around the world.

Published by MQ Publications Limited
12 The Ivories 6–8 Northampton Street London N1 2HY
Tel: 020 7359 2244 / Fax: 020 7359 1616
e-mail: mail@mqpublications.com

Copyright © MQ Publications Limited 2000

Text & Illustrations © Lauren White 2000

ISBN: 1-84072-181-2

1 3 5 7 9 0 8 6 4 2

Printed in Spain